Nature's Children

DOWNY WOODPECKER

Katherine Grier

GROLIER
EDUCATIONAL

FACTS IN BRIEF

Classification of the Downy Woodpecker
- Class: *Aves* (birds)
- Order: *Piciformes* (woodpeckers)
- Family: *Picidae*
- Genus: *Dendrocopos*
- Species: *Dendrocopos pubescens*

World distribution. Exclusive to North America.

Habitat. City suburbs, orchards and woods.

Distinctive physical characteristics. Sharp pointed bill; white back and belly; black wings with white stripes; red spot on the head of the male.

Habits. Mate for life; tap as a means of communication as well as to find food; nest in holes in dead trees; generally lay four or five eggs at a time.

Diet. Insects and some vegetation.

Published originally as
"Getting to Know . . . Nature's Children."

This series is approved and recommended
by the Federation of Ontario Naturalists.

This library reinforced edition is available exclusively from:

GROLIER
EDUCATIONAL

Sherman Turnpike, Danbury, Connecticut 06816

Contents

C

Downy Woodpeckers

Have you ever heard a busy drumming sound coming from a nearby pole or tree? Did you follow it, trying to find out exactly where the sound was coming from? If you did, you might have seen a small, red-headed bird rapping into the wood with its bill. Yes, to us that rapping sound means, "Look, and you'll see a woodpecker!"

Perhaps you've wondered what a woodpecker is doing when it raps or pecks. Why doesn't all that knocking with its bill hurt its head? Maybe you've even thought that woodpeckers weren't quite like other birds—and you would be right.

Woodpeckers are specially suited to life in the trees. We'll find out how by looking at one kind of woodpecker that you are likely to see in your neighborhood, whether you live in the country, town or city. It is a small, lively woodpecker that is not afraid of people. It is called the Downy Woodpecker.

A Long Way Down

A young Downy Woodpecker pokes its head out of the hole in the tree where it was born. It is hungry, but it cannot fly yet. So it is looking for its mother and father who usually feed it. Behind it in the nest, its brothers and sisters call out hungrily too. Where is dinner?

The young Downy sees its parents perched on a distant branch. Why aren't they coming with food? Then suddenly a fly buzzes past. The hungry young Downy cannot resist it. It reaches out to grab this tasty bug snack in its bill and . . . pop! It is out of the nest and fluttering down to the ground. It is the young Downy's first flight!

The Downy Woodpecker parents look on from their perch. They know their young will not leave the nest unless they have good reason to do so. And what better reason is there than food? They watch for the next hungry young bird to try its wings.

Young Downy Woodpeckers.

Downy Relatives

The Downy Woodpecker belongs to a big family. There are 179 different kinds of woodpeckers living around the world. Twenty-two kinds live in North America, and the Downy is one of them.

All woodpeckers have several things in common. They are all good climbers. They all use their bills to poke or dig for their food. And they all can use their bills to make holes for their nests as well.

Just as people look different, so do the Downy's relatives. Some are as big as crows, while others are as tiny as sparrows. Some have bright green feathers, while others are black and white. There are woodpeckers of many other colors as well.

The different kinds of woodpeckers like different things to eat. Many eat insects they find on the ground or in trees. Some lap up the sap that flows from holes they make in tree trunks. And others prefer acorns, storing a supply for the winter in holes they dig in the bark of a tree.

Getting to Know the Downy

The Downy Woodpecker is a small woodpecker. It only weighs about 28 grams (1 ounce) when fully grown. This is about as much as an eraser weighs. The Downy measures about 15 centimetres (6 inches) from its head to the tip of its tail.

The Downy is a handsome bird. It has a bright white chest and a white stripe down its back. It has black wings with white checks and stripes. And the male has a small red patch on the back of its head. The same patch on the female is black or white.

Copycat Cousin

The Downy's distinctive markings should make it easy to recognize. But there is one problem. One of its cousins, the Hairy Woodpecker, has almost the same markings. If you could put a Downy and a Hairy Woodpecker side by side, you would see that the Hairy Woodpecker is much bigger. But since you usually see a woodpecker on its own, this "size test" does not always work.

The best way to tell if a woodpecker is a Downy is to look at its bill. The Hairy Woodpecker's bill is as long as its head, while the Downy Woodpecker's bill is much shorter—about half that length.

Compare this Hairy Woodpecker's bill with that of the Downy. Unlike most woodpeckers, the Downy has quite a short and stubby bill.

At Home on its Range

Downy Woodpeckers live all over North America—that is, wherever there are trees. They make their homes in city parks and backyards, farm orchards and open woodlands.

Every Downy lives on its own range—a large area of land that gives the Downy its food and shelter. In it there are sure to be deciduous trees—trees that lose their leaves in the fall—where the Downy can find insects and grubs to eat. And there will also be dead or dying trees in which the Downy can chisel out a roosting hole to sleep in or a nest hole for its young.

In spring and summer, the Downy shares a range with a mate and raises a family. In fall and winter it lives alone on its own range. The Downy lives on the same range year after year. It gets to know where favorite trees or stumps are, how to get from one spot to another and where the best eating and hiding places are.

Only the males have a patch of red on their heads.

A Friendly Neighbor?

In fall and winter when the Downy lives by itself, it does not get upset if other birds come into its range. In fact, being a small woodpecker among many larger birds, it sometimes does not have much choice.

The Downy and the Hairy Woodpeckers—who look so much alike—sometimes even share the same trees. The larger Hairy Woodpecker searches the main trunk for food and uses its longer, stronger bill to chisel holes in hard live wood. The smaller Downy Woodpecker finds soft dead limbs to dig holes in. It moves easily among the smaller branches looking for insects near the bark's surface. Because the two woodpeckers look for food in different places, the Downy and the Hairy live side by side in peace. A Downy will also share its range with another Downy.

But when a Downy couple start making their nest and getting ready to raise a family, watch out. They are no longer friendly neighbors. In fact they want to be left alone and will drive other birds, even other Downy Woodpeckers, out of their range.

A Downy Diet

The Downy gets much of its food by eating insects that crawl on the bark of a tree. Many insects can move fast, but so can the Downy. It hops quickly over its favorite feeding places—small trees and the upper branches and twigs of big trees—snatching bugs where it finds them. Its favorites are beetles, beetle larvae, ants, caterpillars and other small insects.

The Downy eats some fruits and berries too, when it can find them—raspberries, blackberries, cherries and even the berries of poison ivy and poison sumac. It will also drink sap from the holes that its relative, the Sapsucker Woodpecker, taps deep into live trees.

The Downy's eating habits change with the seasons. In spring and summer there are lots of insects, and it can eat well just by looking for them on top of the bark. But in fall and winter, it must get insects that live under the tree bark, and so it must tap for its meal.

Unlike other woodpeckers the Downy will hunt for food in smaller scrub and bushes.

Tapping for Food

How does the Downy get at insects that live in tunnels in tree wood or telephone poles? First it chisels into the wood to open up the tunnels. It does this by hammering its straight sharp bill into the wood over and over again. Although the Downy's bill is made mostly of hard bone, it is not as long or strong as many other woodpecker's bills. So it usually digs into softer dead or dying wood for an insect dinner.

Getting the insects out of their tunnel homes is no problem either. It uses its tongue to "fish" them out. The Downy's tongue is long enough to probe deep into the insects' tunnels. On the tip of its tongue are tiny barbs that work like a fishhook. When the Downy catches an insect, the barbs hold it fast. Its tongue is also sticky, and this helps hold the insect too. Then the Downy draws its tongue back into its bill with the bug attached.

A Protected Body

Would you rather catch a baseball with your bare hand or a padded glove? Probably a padded glove. The Downy uses padding too. It drums its bill against a tree over 100 times a minute. But its head does not get hurt because it is protected—just as your hand is protected by a baseball glove. The Downy's bill is wide at the base, the bones of its skull are thick and heavy, and the muscles around its head and neck are strong. Together, the bill, skull and muscles spread and absorb the force of the blows to protect the Downy's head from injury.

When the Downy chisels into a tree trunk, the air is filled with fine powder and flying chips of wood. You would think that its nostrils would get clogged, and that it would have a hard time breathing. But the Downy's nostrils, which are at the base of its bill, are covered with fine feathers. These feathers work as a filter and keep out all the wood dust, so that it breathes in only clear air.

The Downy leans on its tail for extra support.

Tree Top Eating

Holding onto a tree and eating at the same time might not sound like your idea of a picnic, but it is a snap for a Downy.

Like most woodpeckers, the Downy is well-equipped for climbing straight up trees. It has four long toes on each foot, two pointing forward and two backward. Each toe ends in a sharp, curved nail that gives the Downy a good grip.

The Downy's tail also helps it both when it is climbing and when it stops to eat. The feathers in its tail are pointed and stiff. The Downy leans back against these stiff tail feathers and uses them as a prop.

Two pairs of toes, one pointing forward and the other back, give the Downy a very firm grip.

The rough bark shown here is easy for a Downy to cling to.

Keeping Clean

The Downy works hard, but it also takes time to relax. Preening and keeping its feathers well tended is one way the Downy takes it easy. Each Downy has a special high stump or tree branch that is its favorite preening place.

There it uses its bill to poke deep down among its feathers, cleaning away dirt and tiny parasites. It straightens some feathers by pulling them carefully through its bill. In between preening, the Downy shrugs its shoulders, fluffing and lifting its feathers before flattening them out again.

No matter how carefully a woodpecker takes care of its feathers, a year's wear-and-tear makes them worn and ragged. And so each summer, the Downy molts—it grows a new set of feathers. The old ones fall out little by little, so that the Downy is never bald. It always has enough feathers to go about its work as the new feathers grow in.

A downy's molt is so gradual it almost passes unnoticed.

Going South?

When winter sets in, most Downy Woodpeckers stay on their own ranges. Their roosting holes are little caves in wood that protect them from the wind, snow and rain. Using their bills, they can tap for insects from inside their cave.

But Downy Woodpeckers that live in places that get very cold or snowy in the winter cannot always find enough to eat. They fly to warmer places where they are sure to find food. Some just move down a mountainside to a protected valley, while others fly farther south.

One bird-watcher found that some Downy Woodpeckers who usually flew south stayed on their ranges all winter when she put suet feeders out for them. The suet was the extra food they needed for the winter.

Some Downy Woodpeckers shift southward in the fall to avoid the colder regions.

Two Kinds of Baths

Downy Woodpeckers do not like water very much, but they do take an occasional bath in the snow. On a warm, sunny day in late winter, you might find one dipping its bill into the wet snow, scooping the snow over its shoulder and flapping its wings to spread it around.

There is one kind of bath that Downy Woodpeckers really like—a sunbath. A Downy will sprawl along a branch, facedown, with its wings spread half-open. It lifts the feathers on its shoulders and neck, sticks its feet straight back out from under it and soaks in the sun's rays.

Warm rays of the sun are a welcomed treat during the long winter.

Woodpecker Talk

The Downy does not "sing" as many birds do. But it does make sounds and movements that tell other birds how it feels and what it is going to do. Some of a Downy's calls are loud and some are soft, others are angry, frightened or happy. Its loud "thick" call says, "Here I am," and can be heard a long way off. A sharp "tick-tick-tick" call says, "I'm a little scared." A loud "tickirrr" call says, "Danger!" A soft "tut-tit-wi-tut-it" call says, "Hello," or, "It's good to be with you."

Sounds are not the Downy's only way of "talking." It also raises and lowers its feathers and flies or moves in different ways to send messages. If a Downy wants to say, "This is my tree. Stay away," it stretches out its head and neck, points its bill into the air and whips its head from side to side. To other birds, the message is clear.

Forest Drums

The Downy does not tap on wood only to find food. Sometimes it uses its bill like a drumstick to rap out messages on favorite hollow posts and trees. It drums in steady bursts. It can rattle off 10 hits in a row and then do it again and again, perhaps 15 times in a minute. In this way it sends messages:

"I'm looking for a mate!"

"This is my part of the woods!"

"I'm over here!"

The rapid tapping of the Downy can be heard for quite a distance.

Time for a Mate

In late winter or early spring, the Downy knows it is time to raise a family. The female begins to look for a mate. She drums out a message and if a male hears her, he drums back.

Before they settle down as a pair, the two Downy Woodpeckers do a lot of drumming back and forth. They also strut around with their feathers fluffed out, and visit nest holes from past years. All this helps them decide to stop living alone and start a family.

Downy Woodpeckers mate for life. They nest on the same range, usually the male's, year after year. But because they live alone the rest of the year, even Downy Woodpeckers who have mated before must get to know each other all over again at the beginning of each nesting season.

Few woodpeckers perch crosswise on a branch like the one shown here. The Downy is the exception.

Hard-working Nest Builders

Downy Woodpeckers dig out a new nest hole each year. They each tap at many different trees before choosing a new site—but the female has the final say.

Downy Woodpeckers dig their holes high above the ground in dead wood. Often the female will choose a dead tree branch, a tall fence post or a telephone pole. The male does most of the chiseling and the female helps. The Downy will dig for about 15 minutes at a time and then take a break to rest or eat before going back to work again.

The Downy Woodpeckers work hard, but they also work carefully. First they dig a small cone in the middle of the spot that will be the "front door." As the hole gets deeper, the digging Downy must wiggle out backward, its feathers all ruffled, to toss a bill-full of wood chips over its shoulder.

Snug and Safe

When the Downy Woodpeckers are finished, they have a nest that will shelter them and their young from bad weather and keep them safe from most enemies. The entrance hole is just big enough to let a grown-up Downy pass through. A passage leads straight in, then drops down to a wide nest hole. A few wood chips are left inside to make the floor soft enough for a nest.

Downy Woodpeckers take about two weeks to dig out their nest hole. But if other birds drive them away close to egg-laying time, they can dig a new nest in two days of *very* hard work.

In between digging, the Downy Woodpeckers drum out the message that the small territory around their nest tree belongs to them and nobody else. And they drive away any bird who comes too close.

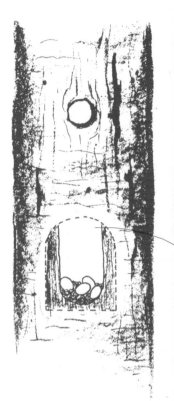

Cut-away of a Downy's nest hole.

A Family on the Way

The Downy female usually lays four or five small eggs. They are pure white, unlike many birds' eggs that are colored or mottled to blend in with the world around them. Because the Downy's eggs are out of sight inside the nest hole, special coloring is not needed to keep them from being seen.

The Downy takes four to six days to lay her eggs. Once she is finished, a peaceful time begins. For 12 days, until the eggs begin to hatch, both parents take long turns keeping the eggs warm and covered. During the whole 12 days, the eggs are never left uncovered for more than a few minutes.

Busy with Babies

The Downy nestlings are blind, featherless and hungry when they hatch. Their parents take turns feeding them. They bring food to the nest every two or three minutes all through the day. While one parent searches for food, the other usually stays with the babies, protecting them and comforting them with soft calls.

At first the parent brings one or two very small ants. It climbs right down into the nesting hole with this snack to feed one helpless baby at a time. But within a week, the nestlings are strong enough to climb the nest walls and meet their parent halfway. By this time they have moved onto big insects. Before long they are chippering loudly at the nest's entrance as they wait for the next delivery of food.

Until the young are grown, the father spends his nights in the nest while the mother sleeps nearby in another roosting hole. The father keeps the nest clean. The babies' droppings come out in tough clean sacks that the father picks up in his bill and dumps outside.

Finding Their Wings

After three weeks of hard work, the Downy Woodpecker parents know that it is almost time for their young to leave the nest. The young woodpeckers are almost as big as their parents and have grown a full set of feathers.

The adults encourage the young ones to leave. They begin to spend much of their time outside the nest. And they bring food only about three times an hour instead of 15 times. At last hunger overcomes the young woodpeckers' fear of flying and soon they are as graceful in the air as their parents.

Not quite ready to fly . . . but it won't be long.

On Their Own

Once the young Downy Woodpeckers have left the nest, they never return to it. Each sleeps alone, hidden among the leaves of a nearby tree.

But they are far from ready for life on their own. Though they learn to fly and climb up trees very quickly, learning to feed themselves takes another three weeks. During that time, their parents help feed them. They find their young by following their calls. Those who are closest or call loudest get fed first.

As the young Downy Woodpeckers get better and better at looking after themselves, the family begins to move apart. By the middle of the summer, the young birds have grown up. They fly off to find ranges of their own and to dig a roosting hole for the coming winter.

As for their parents, they return to their own separate ranges. There they take up their solitary fall and winter ways until spring draws them together again.

Feeding so many young keeps both mom and dad very busy.

A Downy Long Life

The Downy, like most woodpeckers, is a tough bird. It is most in danger when it is young—as an egg, a nestling or a very young bird without a roosting hole. Then animals small enough to sneak into a Downy Woodpecker hole (such as a red squirrel) and hunting birds (such as a hawk) may try to make it into a tender meal.

But the Downy really has few enemies. If it survives the early days, it is quite likely to live to Downy old age—about eight or nine years old. That is not so surprising. After all, the Downy carries all the tools it needs to take care of itself in its life in the trees.

Words to Know

Larvae   The second stage of an insect's life, after it has hatched out of the egg.

Markings   Patterns and colors in fur and feathers.

Mate   To come together to produce young. Also either member of an animal pair.

Molt   To shed feathers or fur from time to time.

Nest hole   A hole dug in a tree by a Downy Woodpecker for a nest.

Nestling   A young bird that has not yet left the nest.

Nostrils   Openings in the nose or bill that allow air into the body.

Parasites   A plant or animal that lives on another.

Preening   Grooming of feathers with the bill.

Range   Area that an animal or group of animals lives in.

Roosting hole   A hole in a tree where a Downy Woodpecker sleeps at night.

INDEX

Cover Photo: Robert McCaw (Network Stock Photo File)

Photo Credits: Brian Morin (Network Stock Photo File), page 4; Michel Bourque (Valan Photos), pages 7, 43; Bill Ivy, pages 10, 13, 26; Harold V. Green (Valan Photos), page 14; Robert McCaw (Network Stock Photo File), pages 17, 30, 34; Stephen J. Krasemann (Valan Photos), page 18; National Museum of Natural Science, page 21; James M. Richards, pages 22, 29, 44; Robert C. Simpson (Valan Photos), page 25; Barry Griffiths (Network Stock Photo File), page 34; Wayne Lankinen (Valan Photos), pages 38, 41.

Printed and Bound in Italy by Lego Sp